The Easy Way To Plan A Church Conference

A step-by-step procedure for
churches of all sizes
and denominations

Revised Edition

Marie Huggins McCurley

DISCLAIMER

The purpose of this book is to give general information. Neither author nor publisher shall have any responsibility or liability to any person or entity with respect to loss or harm allegedly caused directly or indirectly by the information contained in this book. While all attempts have been made to verify information provided in this publication, the publisher assumes no responsibility for errors, omissions, or contrary interpretation of the subject matter.

This book is a work of the author's experience, opinion, and research. Readers are cautioned to rely on their own judgment about their individual circumstances and to act accordingly.

DEDICATION

This book is dedicated to my children (Tanya McCurley Clifton, Kim McCurley, and Kevin McCurley) who never cease to amaze me with their support of whatever I attempt to accomplish.

Table of Contents

Preface

The path that led me to write this book actually began several months after I joined the staff at Rock of Ages Baptist Church, Maywood, Illinois. I was asked to serve on a committee to plan a conference. This conference was especially for girls and women. I had spent many years developing and planning training seminars and workshops, but planning a church conference would be a new experience. This assignment turned out to be very rewarding.

When the conference was over, people continuously asked the committee how they planned such a successful event. On my way home from work one evening, out of curiosity, I stopped at the local library to see if there were any books in print that would help a layman plan a church conference. Much to my surprise, I found very little information. Consequently, I decided to write this book. This book is based mainly on my personal experience.

I feel blessed to have written a book that allows me to help others while receiving so much inner satisfaction. This book includes suggestions and techniques that will guide you through the planning process and through the conference.

Acknowledgments

Primarily, I thank Rev. Marvin E. Wiley, Pastor, Rock of Ages Baptist Church, Maywood, Illinois. Through his preaching and teaching a seed was planted that inspired me to write this book.

I also thank the ladies that served on that planning committee so long ago.

Introduction

Through the years there has been a tradition to set aside several Sundays a year to celebrate and honor men, women, and youth. Due to the desire to offer members more information on health issues, self-awareness, techniques and strategies for personal growth, and dealing effectively with others on a personal and professional level, many churches are changing that one-day service to an all day Saturday or a weekend event. This event can also be used as an annual fund raiser.

During these weekend events, various activities are planned and speakers are invited to speak on various topics. There is a main speaker for the group session and other speakers that facilitate classes or workshops. These events usually begin on Friday night. On Saturday there are classes and/or workshops on various topics that affect the lives of participants and their families. One or two meals can be provided during the conference. The conference concludes on Sunday with a special program during the morning or afternoon service. The conference can also conclude on Saturday

These conferences can be held on site (your church) or at an off-site facility such as a school or hotel. The decision to have the conference on site or off site will be determined by the number of participants you expect to attend and the amount of space available at your church.

The following topics are covered in this book:

Advance decisions

Committee selection and development

Speakers Vendors

Facilities

Publicity

Registration fee

Expense and income

Fund raising profit

Other appropriate topics.

Small and medium-sized churches that don't have a full-time staff to perform the necessary planning will benefit tremendously from this book. Read this entire book before planning your conference. Read it again and highlight the suggestions you want to use. Examples of forms, letters, etc. are in the Appendix.

I have also included a bonus article titled Five Ways to Enhance Your Interpersonal Skills. This article includes five modules: Communicate Clearly, Adjust Your Attitude, Solve Problems, Manage Conflict, and Deal with Difficult People.

The idea to include this article came to me when I was standing in my empty church about 2:30 p.m. one Sunday afternoon. The attendance on any Sunday is approximately 1200 or more between the 8:00 a.m. service and the 11:00 a.m. service. I realized at that moment that members attend church for a short time on Sunday and leave. Many of the members attend midweek Bible Study classes; but many of them go back to their homes, jobs, and communities to live another week before they return for their spiritual teaching.

During that week, along with the preaching and teaching members have received, they need effective interpersonal skills to cope with the interactions of life and to deal with people who know nothing about what they have experienced in church. Because I had been a trainer, I could not miss an opportunity to research and gather the information provided in this article. Even though you may not work on a conference planning committee, or on any committee, I hope you will be able to use the information provided in the article.

If you know of someone who has talked about planning a church conference, please tell them about this book.

Make Advance Decisions

In order to prevent frustration, chaos, confusion and a sometimes unfriendly atmosphere, you will have to make some advance decisions. Select a date. Choose a theme. Appoint and develop a planning committee.

Select a Date

If you are going to use an off-site facility, I suggest that you start planning six months to a year in advance. This is merely a suggestion. You can certainly have a successful conference with shorter planning time. Set your intended date and two alternate dates.

Check with the off-site facilities to see if the dates you want are available. Once you have confirmed the date, send flyers to all churches and other organizations in the community. Include date and name of facility that you will use. Tell them that more information is forthcoming. Hopefully, they will not plan an event on that date.

Choose a Theme

Select a theme that will motivate people to attend. Find suitable scripture. Make sure the theme and scripture are in agreement and are suitable for the conference whether it is a men's conference, women's conference, youth conference, family conference, or a general church conference. Get your pastor's approval of the theme.

Appoint a Committee

When appointing a committee, select members who are willing to work as team players. Take advantage of knowledgeable people in the congregation. There are many professionals and others who will lend their time and talent just for the asking. Ask for volunteers and select a chairperson.

The chairperson should gather information and use the committee as a sounding board for ideas. Committee members should work as a team and carry out the chairperson's instructions when delegated certain jobs. The chairperson should encourage every member of the committee to give ideas and recommendations. The chairperson should report to the pastor to get approval on actions that need attention.

Each member of the committee should be assigned a specific duty such as facility arrangements, registrations, speaker invitations, confirmation letters, love gifts, deadlines, contacting caterers, and anything else pertinent to the conference. Each member delegated a specific task should have a sub-committee to help perform the duties and responsibilities.

Committee meetings should be planned monthly, bi-weekly, and weekly depending on the closeness of the conference date. Develop an agenda and stick to it. Begin the meeting on time. Keep interruptions at a minimum. Encourage the secretary to keep accurate records. At the end of the meeting, the chairperson should summarize the discussion. Review all tasks that need to be completed by each member before the next meeting.

Some churches find it more cost effective to open the church on specific days and certain times. If the open hours of the church are not conducive to the committee's availability, meetings can be held at places other than the church. Always get the pastor's permission before holding a meeting at another place. The chairperson should be the sole person responsible for running the meeting and should make a habit of closing the meeting on time.

Develop the Committee

During the course of planning and preparing for the conference there is bound to be some conflict. Occasionally, because of a lack of effective communication skills, conflict may arise between committee members or eventually with conference participants. The chairperson should seek ways to improve the interpersonal skills of the committee.

One way to do this is to arrange for a trainer to facilitate a workshop where the objectives are to improve the committee's people skills. I have included an article titled Five Ways to Enhance Your Interpersonal Skills in this book that can be developed into a class. If you decide to present a class, ask the entire committee to attend.

Present this class at the beginning of the planning stage, preferably, soon after the committee is selected. This workshop will prepare the committee to relate mutually with various personalities. I have listed several problems sometimes encountered during meetings by members serving as chairpersons.

poor attitudes

non-commitment

one person monopolizing the meeting

demonstrated dislike of other members

private conversations during meeting

Tailor the workshop to address specific needs. If you know of a specific problem that should be addressed, ask the presenter to incorporate the problem and include a suggested solution during the workshop.

While selecting the committee, notify the ushers and greeters of the event. They will not have to attend the meetings but assign someone to inform them of the activities that you want them to participate in.

Develop a Budget

A budget should be established and used as a guideline for making financial decisions. Remember that your budget will be determined by the facility selected and the activities planned. Budgets should project income and expense. Estimate every possible expense and all expected income.

Examples of expenses are facility rental and expenses; speakers' honorariums and expenses; promotions; printing; love gifts for participants; caterers; and marketing. There will be other miscellaneous expenses that you must allow for in your budget. Examples of income are registration fees, vendor fees, and general contributions.

It is important to stay within your budget. Encourage each sub-committee to be cost effective in making their selections. Each sub-committee should make an itemized list of everything they think they need to purchase. After making the list, the chairperson should review the list to see if any items can be eliminated.

Your largest expense will be the cost of a rental facility and catering. This is not true if you have the conference on site. Never purchase services or items without determining where it will be deducted in the budget. If the entire amount allotted in one category is not needed, funds can be shifted to other categories. Your largest income will come from registration fees.

Locate a Facility

Whenever you plan a conference, finding the right facility is one of the factors that help ensure a successful event. In this section, I'll discuss the various facilities such as churches, hotels, and schools and the steps to secure them.

Once you set the date and decide on the site, you should immediately reserve rooms in the church, the hotel, or the school. Call well in advance to secure your projected date. Do not publicize a date until you have a confirmation from the church, hotel or other selected conference site. The conference will appear poorly organized if you promote one date and later have to change.

When selecting a facility, do not select the most expensive place available. Select a facility easy to locate and a place where participants will feel safe. If your church has space, hold the conference there or rent another church. Rental space is less costly for a church facility or a school than for a first-class hotel.

If you decide to use a hotel or school, consider transportation. What is the availability of public transportation? Many prospective participants do not have cars. Will the church provide a bus to transport seniors and others without private transportation? You should also stipulate that parents must accompany their children. You don't want parents to drop their children off and you have to provide transportation and be responsible for them as well.

If the conference is held more than one day and you have overnight lodging, the participants will need some optional activities. The committee will have to plan suitable activities for the evening.

Hotels

All reservations should be made as far in advance as possible. Hotels often reserve space several years in advance. Many hotels can easily accommodate at least 500 participants for a conference. Perhaps members will personally know of hotels that will accommodate your needs. If you are expecting thousands of participants, I suggest you consider a convention center and hire a Certified Meeting Planner

Visit the hotels that you are considering. Make sure they have adequate rooms to serve as classrooms and a large meeting room to hold all participants for prayer and praise service. Inquire about their audiovisual equipment. Meet with the caterer to investigate moderately priced meals. Inquire about parking and whether or not there is a parking fee. If you are using overnight lodging, check the sleeping rooms.

You will need a large meeting room to assemble all participants together for prayer and praise sessions, and to hear the main speaker. This room will be used for meals if required. The large meeting room should allow easy entry and exit. This room should be located if possible, close to restrooms. Inquire about the sound system in this room.

The sales department of the hotel usually handles conferences when sleeping rooms and/or catering is requested. The rate for the large meeting room used for general sessions is sometimes based on the number of sleeping rooms and/or smaller meeting rooms to be used as classrooms.

Hotel Catered Meals

Hotels make a large percentage of their revenue on the sale of food, so they sell catered meals along with their large meeting rooms. When preparing for the conference, decide whether you will have catered meals or if participants will be responsible for their own meals. Most of the time if meals are catered, the large meeting room is reserved for you at no cost. Keep constant communication with the hotel. Record the name of the sales representative with whom you've made arrangements so when questions arise, you'll have a direct contact.

When you receive the booking contract, review it for accuracy. If there are any errors, contact the hotel representative immediately. Sign and return the contract promptly. Keep a copy for your records. Deposits will vary from hotel to hotel. Make a careful note of the cutoff date the hotel needs final confirmation. Cancel all rooms you will not use. If the hotel is not notified timely, you may have to pay for rooms that you will not use.

Most hotels require a final count for meals several days before the conference. This final count means you guarantee to pay for a certain number of meals. It does not matter whether you have the number of participants to eat the meals or not, you will be charged for them. If you plan to use a hotel, ask the committee to visit at least three and get bids. Discuss options with the pastor to decide which hotel will best serve your needs.

Hotel Rooms Used For Classes

Check the size, lighting, and temperature control in the rooms that will be used for classrooms. The size of the classroom will depend on how many participants registered for each class. You will not know how many rooms at the time you reserve the rooms, but you can reserve rooms with a maximum in mind. If you have the conference at the church, some will register the day of the conference. If the conference is held at a hotel, I do not encourage same day registration. It will be too chaotic.

If you are providing meals, at this time, a number has been confirmed. It is not easy to add additional meals on the same day; but, if you have paid for meals and do not have the participants to eat them, I suggest that you register on the day of the conference. Adjustments will have to be made in the classrooms.

Give the hotel the following information:

Date(s) of the conference

Set up for each room

Number of meals required

Training aids needed in each room

Questions to ask the hotel representative:

1. What is the cost for a large meeting room? (Give the hotel the projected number of participants.)

2. What is the cost for smaller rooms that can be used for classrooms?

3. What is the cost of sleeping rooms?

4. Will the facility provide use of a large meeting room at no cost if you purchase meals?

5. What kind of audio technology is available in the large meeting room?

6. Is there a control in the room for heat and/or air conditioner?

7. Where are the electrical outlets in the classrooms and large meeting room?

8. Where are the restrooms?

9. Can the large meeting room be darkened to show a film?

10. Where can you place the head table? How many seats?

11. Will the head table be on a riser?

12. Is there parking for participants? If so, is there a cost?

13. Are decorations allowed? If so, what kind?

14. What are the menus?

15. When is deadline for the final count for meals?

16. What is the amount of deposit needed to hold space?

17. When is balance due?

18. What is the date that you can cancel with no penalty?

19. Where can you place the vendors?

Schools

If you are considering using a school, ask a committee member to make a visit to determine if it is suitable for your needs. Thoroughly investigate the school to see if it meets your requirements. Request an application for rental. Applications are usually sent to the school board for final approval. Submit your application early.

Some questions to ask school representative:

☐ Is the date selected available?

☐ What is cost of rental?

☐ Is there an hourly rate or flat rate?

☐ How many rooms are available for use?

☐ Can your caterer use the kitchen?

☐ Will the cafeteria be available for catered meals?

☐ How many chairs or desks in rooms?

☐ Can you move chairs from room to room?

☐ What entrances and exits can be used?

☐ Where are restrooms located?

☐ How many custodians will be on duty?

☐ Is the cost of the custodians included in the rental rate?

☐ What time will the school be opened and closed?

- ☐ Can the auditorium be used?
- ☐ How many seats are in the auditorium?
- ☐ Is there a sound system and microphone available?
- ☐ Can you bring in a sound expert?
- ☐ Can you use their piano and/or organ?
- ☐ Will the school provide security? If so, is the cost included in the quoted rate?
- ☐ Will you have to provide liability insurance? If so, how much?

On Site

If you decide to hold the conference at your church, make sure you have adequate space. The classrooms should have privacy. The rooms should be far enough apart so participants in one room cannot hear what is being said in another room. If you have only one or two rooms that can be used, do not move participants between classrooms, let the speakers move from room to room. If you have to use the same room, plan frequent breaks and after each break ask participants to sit in a different seat. This gives them a chance to interact with other members of the conference and sometimes breaks up private conversations that have developed.

Contract with a caterer to provide meals. Choose an inexpensive caterer that will provide a delightful menu suitable for participants in a training class.

Negotiate with caterer to get a reasonable price per person.

Catered Meals at Church or School

When using a catering service, several details have to be ironed out during the advance decision making. Select a caterer that you have used before or one that is highly recommended by the committee responsible for meals.

Menus should be light. Serve a continental breakfast that consists of small pastries, bagels, fruits, juices, coffee, milk and tea. The lunch menu can be a variety of salads, fruits, cheeses, mini sandwiches, Jell-O, coffee, tea, and soft drinks. Foods like the above will help ensure alertness in the classes. I've noticed when you serve a heavy meal for lunch and classes are scheduled for the afternoon, the participants' energy level drops far too low.

Some Questions to Ask Caterer:

- ❐ How many people can they accommodate?
- ❐ Do they need to use the kitchen?
- ❐ Will they clean up after meals?
- ❐ What time should the serving space be available?
- ❐ Will they serve the entire audience at once or will they serve in shifts?
- ❐ What is the amount of deposit? When is it due?

Select Topics

Choose topics that interest your prospective participants. Distribute a questionnaire to the congregation to be returned in two weeks. The quick return will show you how hungry members are for useful information.

List all topics that will address the needs of prospective participants. Be sure to include old and new topics that respond to pressing needs and issues. If you promote only old topics, many prospective participants will not attend because they may have heard presentations on old issues during past conferences.

Plan to have activities for the children and the teenagers. For the children, consider a puppet show, clowns, stories and games. Encourage all children to participate in the activities. If feasible, serve their meals in a separate area. It will appear to them that they are having their own conference.

Teenagers have special needs. They go through crises daily. Peer pressure, poor communication skills, low self-esteem, and stressed parent-child relationships are just a few of their problems. In some communities introduction to drugs and pressure to join gangs is prevalent. Also, include topics that address school information such as college preparation and entrance. Ask the pastor to determine, from questionnaires, topics that should be addressed. (Sample questionnaire in Appendix)

Select Speakers

Ask your pastor to select speakers. Pastors usually have current information on speakers that they prefer. The pastor should always select the main speakers. Highlight the main speakers in your publicity.

Ask deacons, mothers, ushers, choir members or any church member to recommend speakers for classes. Create a speakers database. List name, church affiliation, address, where you heard him/her speak, date and topic. The data will become priceless when a speaker is needed for future events.

Investigate referred speakers. Contact those that share similar beliefs. Do not bring in someone who will use your conference as a forum to spread his or her doctrine. Do you have speakers in your congregation? Is your congregation biased against using members of the church? Is the only true expert the one that comes from afar? There is value in using your own members to speak on certain topics. One problem that may occur is finding out who the good speakers are. If your church has a data profile on each member, this will be an easy task.

Contact speakers immediately and tell them exactly what you want. Speakers usually fill calendars six months to one year in advance. If you personally know a speaker, pick up the phone and call him or her. If you do not know the speaker, write a letter. Whether you phone, fax, email, or mail a letter, provide the same information. In the event that you send a letter, indicate that you will follow up with a phone call when the speaker has had a chance to review the letter.

Inform the speakers of the conference dates, time and length of class, topic you want addressed, and whether the speaker should expect questions after the presentation. If you have special topics with an outline and all the required material prepared, let the speakers know. Find out if the speakers have material on the topic you want him or her to present; if they do, request their outline and a list of training aids they will need.

Training aids are:

> overhead projector, screen, DVD, TV
>
> laptop, white board, easel, flip chart
>
> markers, erasers, video, etc.

If you want to review the topic, state a deadline for the outline to reach you. From the outline, extract a short description of the topic to use in your publicity. Before participants register, they like to know the objectives of the classes. The description will help the participants determine if the class will be beneficial. If the speakers don't have materials such as books, articles, etc., you can provide.

Most speakers prefer to provide their own material. If you have to provide the material, send it well in advance so speakers will have sufficient time to prepare a good presentation. Once the speakers accept, send confirmation letters outlining all the points you have previously discussed. Ask the main speaker to send you a short biography and a picture.

Some speakers will require an honorarium. Others will be glad to participate for no fee and will be surprised later to receive a love offering. If you really want the speaker that requires an honorarium, emphasize the fact that your budget is limited and you cannot afford a large amount. State what you can afford. Speakers will sometimes agree to lower their usual honorarium or eliminate the fee because they count on getting other speaking opportunities from conference participants. Their presentation will be publicity for them.

Expert speakers from community organizations, health agencies, financial institutions, and other entities are sometimes available at no cost. Call your local chamber of commerce to find out what agencies are located in your community. (Sample of confirmation letter in Appendix)

Publicize

The type of publicity or promotion will depend on the number of participants that you want to attract. If you expect the immediate congregation and a few friends to attend, circulate flyers and make weekly announcements.

If you desire to make it an open event, you have several options. Radio, TV, local cable, newspaper ads, bookstores, record stores, and direct mailing. By all means, use the social networks like facebook, twitter, and any others. After each conference, add the participants' names and addresses to your database and you will have your own mailing list available for future events.

Advertising Options Television and Radio

Airtime is very expensive. Poll your congregation to see if someone works for the media. It's possible that you may be able to get free advertising. If not, you may find it more cost-effective to advertise through the local cable stations and radio stations that air religious programs. Cable television stations usually run public service announcements on a community access channel.

Newspapers

Placing an ad in a newspaper is an effective way of promoting your conference, but is also quite expensive. When you want to reach an audience in a certain area, local newspapers will usually run articles on special events at little or no cost. You can send information in as a Press Release.

Direct Mail

Collect business cards and vendor information. Develop a database of churches that visit. Add to the list neighbors, friends, and relatives that may be interested in the conference. Once you have identified your prospective participants, you can develop your mailing list. If your budget is large enough, and you want to reach a large audience, you can rent mailing lists for certain geographical areas. You can also purchase mailing lists.

Christian Bookstores and Record Stores

Ask bookstores and record stores to display posters and pass out flyers to their customers. To those that honor your request, give one free registration or a discount on one registration.

Word of Mouth

Don't forget the congregation. Have the publicity committee talk it up. If you want to include churches that you occasionally fellowship with, have the committee contact those churches.

Internet

Most homes have access to the Internet. Many churches have Web Sites. List your conference on the Internet. This is a cost-effective way to reach a large audience. Any promotional activity should include the theme; the date(s) and time of the conference; the location; main speakers; registration fee; what you will receive with the registration; list of classes or workshops; contact person; telephone number and deadline for registration.

When you expect participants from out of town and no one is available to give information, put hotel information and/or travel information and rates on a voice mail message. Include name and phone numbers of hotels that will give special rates to participants if they mention they are attending the conference.

Determine Registration Fee

The cost per participant will vary depending on whether the conference is held off-site or on-site. List all expenses such as cost of facility rental including any sleeping rooms, catering, honorarium for speakers, love gifts, promotions, decorations, printing, and transportation. To this cost add the projected profit for the fund-raiser. To arrive at the conference fee, divide the total expenses by the number of projected participants. (See example in Appendix)

Ask selected ministries to pay half the registration fee for seniors or give seniors a discount. Lower the fee for children and give a discount when more than one child from a family registers.

Method of payment

When promoting the conference, state the payment options. Begin your payment plan as soon as you set the date for the conference. If the conference is to be small, make the payment schedule fit the needs of your congregation. Always set a deadline. Many participants will pay in full. Others will pay weekly or biweekly.

Some prospective participants live on a monthly fixed income and will pay monthly. Decide whether a payment plan is feasible. Set your payment dates so you will receive enough money to cover all deposits before the deadlines set by the facility and the caterer.

If the conference is open to the public, you will receive payments by mail. In this case, request full payment from everyone and acknowledge receipt of payments. Specify the last date to cancel and the date for return of refund. All payments should be received at least 30 days before the date of conference.

Notify Vendors

Decide early what products and/or services will be exhibited. Cosmetics, Bibles, books, clothing, jewelry, videotapes, audiotapes, and services can be exhibited. If this is a large conference, vendors will travel from far and near.

If your conference is small now, don't worry, each year it will grow. Send vendors an application and a restriction list that includes a space for signature. This will show agreement to the restrictions. Booths should be assigned based on receipt of vendor application and fee. (Sample vendor letter and vendor form are in the Appendix.)

Place vendors in an area that will be easily accessible to the participants. Place a chair at each booth unless they request more. Many vendors bring tables, racks and chairs.

Sample Vendor Restriction List

All vendors are restricted to a designated area.

Vendors are responsible for their employees.

Excessive noise and flashing lights are not

allowed in the exhibit area.

Open and close at designated time.

Select Love Gifts

The purpose of giving love gifts is to show appreciation to participants who attend the conference. Decide early what you want to purchase so the cost can be included in the registration fee. Items you can purchase are tote bags, tee shirts, caps, pens, jackets, and cups. Purchase whatever your budget will allow. Some vendors give discount prices if you purchase large quantities. If you purchase a large quantity, develop a plan for disposal of leftover items or do not date items and you will be able to use them at a later date.

Poll your congregation to see if any members or members' employers will donate items. Write a letter to companies, especially vendors you do business with, and ask for promotional samples. In the letter state your purpose, date of conference, and the number of participants expected to attend. You will be surprised at the response. Companies love to give promotional samples to a large population at one time. This is free advertisement for them. Locate space to store items until the date of conference. (Sample letter to companies in Appendix)

Prepare For Class Registration

After receiving confirmation of topics from speakers, distribute class registration forms along with the registration package. On each registration form, list alternate classes in case of low registration in a particular class. Use the computer to make a registration data sheet for each class. If you do not have a computer, design the registration form by some other means. Make a list with maximum seats in a class. As the registration forms arrive, add the names to the appropriate class list. When you reach the maximum, begin another list.

You will have extremely high registrations for some classes and low registrations in others. In the event of high registrations, plan two or three sessions on the same topic. At this time you should know how many classrooms you will need, the size of the rooms and how many participants will be in each room.

If a speaker is presenting an active training class, you should register at least seven participants to have a productive class. If the class is interactive, I prefer a maximum of thirty-five participants. The maximum in a lecture class can be larger depending on method of presentation, the size of the room and the sound system.

Notify speakers as soon as possible regarding the number of sessions and participants in each session so speakers can prepare handouts accordingly. If you are at a hotel or school locate the copy machine and find out the cost per copy. Some of the speakers may need additional copies of handouts due to last minute registration. If a copy machine is not available to make copies for additional participants, ask the speaker to give you a master copy and you promise to mail each participant a copy after the conference. Keep your promise.

Classroom Setup

Your class registration will determine the room setup. Listed below are three basic set-ups that can be used for all your classrooms.

1. U-Shaped: Tables are arranged in a U with chairs on the outside facing in. I recommend this style for groups of twenty or less where interaction is expected.

2. Classroom: Several rows of tables usually with an aisle down the middle, with chairs behind the tables all facing the front of the room. This set up is best suited for lecture type presentations where note taking is expected. Groups of up to forty can benefit from this setup.

3. Theater style: Rows of chairs where all are facing the front. This style is suitable for groups of fifty or more where participants are not expected to do anything but listen.

Be sure to confer with your speakers to determine which style they prefer. Speakers will vary in the way they want the classroom set up. There is no right or wrong way; it is strictly up to the speaker.

Weekend Conference

Friday night will be the first night of the conference. Register participants as they arrive and distribute conference bags. Registration should be done in a large room where the participants can move from one table to another to receive various items without causing congestion in any area.

Set up tables and distribute the conference bags. One way to keep ahead of the crowd is to prepare conference bags in advance. Sub-committee members can fill bags prior to conference for those that register early. Only the bags for late registrants will need to be prepared

Conference bags can include:

- ❏ Conference program
- ❏ Love gifts
- ❏ Pocket folder
- ❏ Note paper/pen/pencil
- ❏ Floor plan of facility
- ❏ Class schedule
- ❏ Name badge
- ❏ Evaluation form
- ❏ Certificate of Attendance (optional)

If you permit registration and payment on opening night, set up a special table away from the flow of traffic. Registrations on that night will assure you that you will need to make additional copies of handouts for some speakers. Inform speakers that participants have increased in number. Make sure there is adequate seating in the rooms where you have added participants. This information can also be used for a Saturday only conference.

Conference Program

Typeset your program accurately. If you can afford to send the program to a professional printer, please do. Develop a proofreading team to ensure that all errors are corrected. The creativity and accuracy of the program will have a great impact on your participants.

Factor in breaks, lunch hour and fellowship times. If your conference is held at a hotel or school, allow for travel time if the classrooms are far apart. Set specific times and adhere to them. In order to show fairness and respect to participants and speakers, encourage all involved to be punctual. Begin and end classes on time.

Friday Night Opening Session

Begin on time. The main speaker for the opening session should be one who is well known to the congregation and the community, and who is known to give a power packed enthusiastic delivery. The music ministry or invited guests can provide songs of praise. Have a regular devotion period with prayer and scripture.

Allow approximately thirty-five to forty-five minutes for the main speaker to present topic. The opening session with prayer, praise, devotion, and the main speaker should not exceed ninety minutes. This is only a suggestion. Give highlights of the next day's events and dismiss.

Saturday

Arrive early on the day of the conference. Double-check all arrangements. Have your committee check classroom set-ups, training aids, room temperature, and signs on classroom doors identifying topics. Check the sound system in the large meeting room. Double check any other systems that should be in place.

Breakfast can be served in a large room at the church; the cafeteria in a school; or in the large meeting room at a hotel. If breakfast is served in the large meeting room at a hotel, the Morning Prayer and Praise service can be held in the same room.

Morning Prayer and Praise

Allow approximately twenty to thirty minutes for prayer and praise service. During this session, give instructions for the day. Go over floor plan if conference is at a school or hotel.

Tell participants where hall monitors will be stationed to help them locate classrooms. Remind hall monitors to stay at their posts until ten minutes after the classes have begun. Tell the participants where the restrooms are located and what time and where lunch will be served.

Remind speakers to begin their classes on time and end on time. Tell participants where to assemble for the closing session. I highly recommend beginning early on Saturday and presenting all the classes before serving lunch.

Closing session

Begin on time. The afternoon session will have a devotional period and a presentation from a well-known guest speaker with a spiritual, inspirational, or motivational topic. Allow the speaker approximately thirty-five to forty-five minutes.

After the speaker, the chairperson should introduce the committee, thank participants for attending, and ask that evaluations be left in a designated place. Invite everyone to attend next year. The pastor or pastor's appointee should make the closing remarks, if possible.

Evaluations

Evaluation forms are distributed to each participant to collect information that will determine what areas of the conference need improvement. When you review the evaluations, remain impartial. Remember that each comment reflects the personality of the participant who completes it. Don't be upset if every participant does not have raving reviews for the classes, food, speakers, location, etc.

Use the evaluations to help you determine the attitudes and needs of the participants. The evaluations will also help you expand the topics and offer more of what participants want during future conferences.

Saturday Only Conference

If you plan a Saturday only conference, follow the suggestions given for Saturday in the Weekend Conference information.

After Conference

Immediately send a story about your successful conference to your local newspapers. By all means send a thank you letter to your speakers and include an honorarium if possible. Tell them how much you appreciated their contributing their time and talent to make the conference successful. (Sample speaker thank you letter in Appendix.)

Follow-up Meeting

The chairperson should schedule a follow-up meeting within two weeks of the conference. Ask all committee members to attend. At this meeting, review the evaluations, discuss concerns, and make recommendations for the next conference.

The committee deserves recognition for the work that they did. Give a small reception or send each a letter of commendation. Let them know their work was appreciated.

Bonus Article

Five Ways to Enhance Your Interpersonal Skills

By

Marie Huggins McCurley

Effective interpersonal skills are seriously needed when you work with people. You must be able to adapt your style to work with other personalities. You don't necessarily have to build a lasting relationship with all the participants that attend the conference, nor with the committee members; but, you want to be able to communicate effectively to solicit their help and cooperation.

When I first became a staff member at the church, I was surprised to see conflict arise occasionally within various ministries. I had been a bench member most of my adult life and I was unaware of such behavior. For a long time, I thought the church was the one place where everyone lived by the golden rule. It soon became evident to me that people are just people whether they are in the home, workplace, community, nightclub, or in the church. They all have different philosophies and occasionally disagree on certain ideas.

The above observation was another reason I researched, gathered information and wrote this article. It can be used as an outline to develop the committee or presented as a topic for the conference.

This article titled, Five Ways to Enhance Your Interpersonal Skills gives a brief overview of the following topics: Communicate Clearly, Adjust Your Attitude, Manage Conflict, Solve Problems and Deal with Difficult People.

Communicate Clearly

When interacting with others, you should be able to express

yourself clearly and honestly. Anyone listening to you should have no question as to what you mean. Being clear is not easy; therefore, speaking precisely has to be practiced.

Anytime you communicate, you use your eyes, voice, words, and some sort of body language. You also communicate with the clothing you wear. Your overall appearance makes a profound statement. Another communication skill that is often overlooked and needs attention is listening. Do you just hear words, or do you really listen? I mean do you use a process of thinking or reasoning while listening to get the true meaning out of what is being said? Here is a discussion of the above skills.

Eyes

Where do you look when you are communicating with others? Maintain good eye contact but don't stare at the other person. Don't look at the floor or over the person's shoulder. Don't roll your eyes if you disagree with another's words. Remember that you disagree with what is being said, not with the person. During your next conversation, observe the eye contact made by others. Notice whether you feel intimidated or involved.

Become aware of your eyes during communication. If you think you need to improve your eye contact skills, work on it. Habits can be changed with practice and perseverance.

Words

What words do you use to express your ideas or to make a point? Use simple words that project the clearest understanding. It is not necessary to demonstrate your big word vocabulary. Above all, do no use profanity. Using profanity gives the impression that your vocabulary is very limited and you have to use fillers to express yourself. Words can provoke anger or words can soothe. Choose words carefully. Remember, once a word is out, you can't take it back.

Voice

Do you have a soft quiet voice or a strong loud voice? Both types need to be adjusted. If your voice is soft and quiet, some people tend to not listen or think you are weak or unbelievable. If your voice is strong and loud, some people tend to think you are aggressive and domineering.

You should practice the speed and tone of your voice. The tone you use while communicating is very important and may determine whether or not you get a favorable response. Make an audio tape of yourself speaking. Ask relatives or friends to give you feedback on your voice. Also, the next time you feel angry, make a conscious effort to keep your voice and tone natural.

Body Language

Do you know what type of non-verbal messages you send with your body language? Do you know that body language often speaks louder than words? When I conducted training classes, I could tell the energy level of the class by their body language that included facial expressions and posture. Sometimes the audience was erect and alert and at other times, depending on the time of day and the meal they had consumed, they were slouched and inattentive. I projected my voice and tone according to the body language I read.

Make sure your body language expresses the image you want to convey. Adjust your body language so that it shows enthusiasm and interest. If you read concern on the face of the person you are communicating with, reflect that feeling. Ask if it's something that you've said that is causing the reaction that you are observing. This will give the other person a chance to tell you what has triggered the expression.

Appearance

There is a time and a place for everything. The only advice I have is to dress appropriately for the occasion. Many conferences have color schemes that the committee is asked to adhere to.

Listening

It takes effort and discipline to listen attentively to a speaker. There are many distractions that go on while we are trying to listen. Sometimes there are noises or other conversations going on. You may be preoccupied with the thought of chores left undone and the dog that needs to go out. Numerous things keep us from truly listening.

Make an extra effort to keep distractions to a minimum while you are listening. If you don't understand, clarify with the speaker. Don't be afraid to ask the speaker to define or repeat what he or she has said. Summarize the thought in your own words to see if you got the message correctly.

When you listen, learn to reflect the speaker's feeling when you are confirming what has been said. To listen carefully means to take all components into consideration such as voice, words, eye contact, and body language. If you truly listen, you will make the proper response.

Adjust Your Attitude

There are many factors that determine our attitudes. Our families, teachers, social environment, careers, life experiences, and churches are just a few things that help form our attitudes. Attitudes are also the results of successes, failures, and the way people have reacted to us in the past. Attitudes can change depending on what's going on in our lives at a particular time.

Some of us have health, financial, relationship, and other problems that have an impact on the way we treat others. If we are told that we have an attitude, we should find out what message we are sending and make an effort to adjust it. Many times we are not aware that we are acting in a negative way.

Ways to Adjust Your Attitude

Put aside your need to control and be liked.

Set goals and do things to elevate your self-esteem.

Don't focus on your problems.

Develop a plan and take steps to solve your problems.

Write a brief honest description of your image of yourself. Ask your relatives or friends if they agree with your description. If they don't agree, ask for their description. Don't become defensive and hostile if they don't agree with you. Evaluate their comments, decide what area you want to change, and work on it.

Manage Conflict

We all have had or will have conflict during our daily living. Conflict begins early in life. Toddlers and parents have conflict about eating and sleeping hours. Children have conflict with each other while engaging in play. Teenagers have conflict with parents regarding curfews, dating, friends, and other things that affect their lives. Husbands and wives have conflict regarding children, finances, chores, etc. Teachers have conflict with students regarding homework and class behavior.

We cannot escape conflict. When one or more persons are involved in any communication, there is bound to be some type of conflict. Conflict can impede progress or cause destruction; however, it also has benefits. It can produce interest and arouse curiosity.

Seven Steps to Manage Conflict Listen to the other person's view before responding. Don't purposely try to make the other person angry. State your concerns in a quiet and calm manner. Admit to any mistakes you have made. Handle the other person's mistake with care. If the situation cannot be resolved, ask others for help. Try not to lose friendship over a conflict.

Solve Problems

Solving problems may seem difficult, but if you try the method below, you may find it easy. Eliminate all symptoms and determine what the problem really is. Describe the problem clearly. Use words that are clear and to the point. Power Think to find solutions. Power thinking means to make a list of as many solutions as possible, no matter how ridiculous they may seem. Eliminate the impossible and improbable solutions.

Review the list and cross out the ones that do not have consequences that you can live with at this time. Review the solutions that are left and decide which solution has consequences that you can live with easily. If the solution involves others, decide if they can live easily with the solution. All parties involved should be satisfied. Implement the solution. If all involved agree, put the solution in motion.

Evaluate the solution. After a reasonable amount of time, evaluate the solution. If it is not working, Power Think again, and begin the process over again.

If you have a way of solving problems that works for you, by all means, continue to use it. These are just suggestions.

Deal with Difficult People

When you are interacting with people, who talk constantly, argue consistently, seek approval regularly, or blame others for everything negative that happens, there are effective ways to deal with them.

Talk Constantly

This person seems to know everything. When someone talks to the extent that others have little chance to contribute, calmly explain that others may have something to offer to the discussion. Thank him or her for the contribution and restate some of the important points that were made. Try to make this person comfortable and not ashamed.

Argue Consistently

This person may argue to get attention. He or she may have a mountain of personal problems and not know how to deal with them. When the person argues or becomes aggressive, you must remember to control your temper. Try to find some value in what has been said.

Encourage the person to relax and think in a positive manner. If this does not work, have a private chat with the person to let them know that their actions are affecting the group. The person may have no idea that his or her actions are disturbing. You may find out that this person has personal issues that may need addressing by the pastor or by a social service agency that addresses the specific problem.

Seek Approval Regularly

The reasons for someone always seeking approval could be that he or she has low self-esteem. They may have a need to be right. You must, if possible, avoid taking sides with this person. Encourage others to voice their opinions so there are several opinions on the table for discussion. Give suggestions on how to set goals and build self-esteem to the entire group.

Always blaming others

Some people are uncomfortable with the fact that they make mistakes, too. They are usually afraid to take any kind of risk. When they blame or accuse others of negative actions, ask for the facts to back up the allegations. If you do this consistently, it may discourage this action.

Afterword

I've shared with you all the information I have on planning a church conference. In the bonus article, I have given you suggestions on how to enhance the interpersonal skills of the committee you select. Use what you need and file the rest for a future date.

If you decide to plan a conference after reading this book, you know you're in for lots of work. If you've had this dream for sometime, you can take action and move your dream into reality. There will be some real trying moments so engage the help of a committee that is willing to work as a team and watch your planning come into realization. In the end, the rewards will be great. We did it...so can you.

Appendix

Sample Questions for Questionnaire

1. What problems inhibit your personal success? Be specific.

2. What is the single most significant problem you have in your professional life right now?

3. Have you suffered a tragedy?

4. Do you need college information?

5. Are you planning to start a business in the future?

6. Do you need information on raising children?

7. Are you caring for aging parents?

8. Do you have a teenage parent in the home?

9. Do you want to know how to deal with substance abuse?

10. Do you need information on financial planning?

11. Would you like information on specific health issues?

Sample Speaker Confirmation Letter

Date

Name Address

City/State/Zip

Dear

We are delighted that you have agreed to speak on (topic) at our Annual (Name of Conference) to be held on (date) at (place of conference). The time allotted for this subject is ( ) minutes. If you have materials on this topic, please forward a topic outline. Please let us know if we need to supply you with any reference materials.

We will notify you of your class time and the room you will use as soon as it is established. If you need copies made of your handouts, we will be glad to make them for you. Also, let us know if you need any training aids such as flip charts, TV, DVD, computer, overhead projector, etc.

Please send us your biography and a picture to be used in the publicity of the conference. Again, thank you and we look forward to hearing from you.

Sincerely,

(Name) Conference Chairperson

Sample Letter to Businesses

Date

Company Address

City, State, Zip

Dear Sir or Madam:

(Name of Church) is preparing for its annual (women's, men's, youth) conference to be held (Month, day, year). We are expecting approximately (number expected) participants.

Please send us any samples of products or information that we can give to our participants as love gifts. We will appreciate any donations. We also thank you for your timely response to this request.

Sincerely,

(Name) Conference Chairperson

Sample Letter to Vendors

Date

Company/Church

Address

City, State, Zip

Dear

(Name of Church) is having a (women's, men's, youth) conference on (month, day, year) at (place of conference). We invite you to reserve a booth to display your product(s)/service. Vendors will be able to display their products/services from (state beginning time to ending time) on (specify dates).

If you desire to reserve a table/booth, please complete the enclosed Vendor Form and return it to us with your check by (date). Space is limited so please reply immediately.

Sincerely,

(Name) Conference Chairperson

Enclosure: Vendor Form

Sample Vendor Form

(Name of Church)   (Name of Conference)

Name of Vendor:

_____

Address:

_____

City/State/Zip:

_____

Contact Person:

_____

Product/Service:

_____

Number of booths: _____x (amount)
=_____ (Each booth is $?? each per day)

You may exhibit your products/services from (state beginning and ending time) on (specify date(s). Please sign and return this form to the church office by (specify date) in order to reserve your booth(s).

NOTE: We will not be responsible for any lost or damaged items before, during, or after the conference.

_____

Signature   Date

Example Fee Calculation

Expenses

Facility Rental 1,200.00

Caterer... 1.400.00

Love Gifts ($5.00 Each) 1,000.00

Printing 200.00

Photographer... 150.00

Security.. 200.00

Speakers Honorarium 1,000.00

Projected Fund Raising Profit 5,000.00

TOTAL $10,150.00

200 Projected Participants

$10,150 ÷ 200 = $50.75

You can make Registration Fee $50.00 per adult person.

Sample Evaluation

Name (optional)

Address (optional)

Phone No. (optional)

1. What is your opinion of the price of the conference? Please circle one.

   About right   A little low   Too high

2. What was the most valuable thing you learned today?

3. What other topics would you like to hear?

4. How would you rate the classes? Please circle one.

   Excellent   Fair   Poor

5. How would you rate the speakers? Please circle one.

   Excellent   Fair   Poor

6. Was the length of the class adequate?

7. Was the space sufficient?

8. Would you recommend the conference to others?

9. How did you like the facility?

10. Were the meals adequate?

Sample Thank You Letter to Speakers

Date

Name Address

City/State/Zip

Dear

Thank you for that powerful presentation administered to the participants at our (name of conference) on (date). They were indeed blessed/encouraged by your enthusiastic delivery.

We are so glad that you took time from your busy schedule to share much needed information with us.

Again, thank you and may you continue to be blessed.

Sincerely,

(Name) Conference Chairperson

About the Author

Marie Huggins McCurley is a retired speaker, trainer, consultant and author. Her first published work was in 2000. She is a long time member of the Rock of Ages Baptist Church. She spent many years working in the fields of human and social services. As a trainer, she taught interpersonal skills. Many of her workshops included Solving Problems, Dealing with Difficult People, Communicating Clearly and Integrity. Through those experiences, she learned to interact and assess many different personalities. She has a passion for the spoken and written word. All of her books and articles are published by TKK Publishers.

Resources

Bolton, Robert, Ph.D., People Skills (Simon & Shuster, Inc., New York, New York, 1986)

Bramson, Robert, Coping With Difficult People (Ballantine Books, New York, 1981)

Cava, Roberta, Difficult People (Firefly Books, Inc., Buffalo, New York, 1997)

Colby, Lincoln H., CMP, Editor, The Convention Liaison Council Manual. A Working Guide for Effective Meetings and Conventions (Sixth Edition, Convention Liaison Council, Washington, DC 20005, 1994)

Diehm, William J., Sharpen Your People Skills (Broadman & Holman Publishers, Nashville, Tennessee, 1996)

Karasik, Paul, How to Make it Big in the Seminar Business (McGraw Hill, Inc., New York, NY, 10020, 1981)

Lord, Robert W., Running Conventions, Conferences, and Meetings (Amacom, New York, NY 10020, 1981)

Montgomery, Rhonda J. and Sandra K. Strick, Meetings, Conventions, Expositions, an Introduction to the Industry (Van Nostrand Reinbold, New York, NY 10003, 1995)

Morris, Lois B., and John Oldham, Personality Self-Portrait (Bantam Books, New York, New York, 1990)

Morris, Margie, Volunteer Ministries: New Strategies for Today's Church (Newton-Cline Press, Sherman, TX 75090, 1990)

Singletary, Milly, The Party Planner (Sunset Publication, Honolulu, HI, 1994)

ISBN: 978-0615617886

Thank you for reading this book. I hope you have read something that you can use in planning your event. This book can also be used to plan a family reunion.

Please tell your friends and family about this book and be sure to look for other books published by TKK Publishers. Thanks again!

www.ingramcontent.com/pod-product-compliance
Lightning Source LLC
Chambersburg PA
CBHW071935020426
42331CB00010B/2883